Risk Management

Cheat Sheet

Muhammad Zeeshan Ali, PMP, PMI-ACP

Saqib Javed John, PMP, PMI-ACP, ITIL

Publications
2020

All inquiries should be addressed to (e-mail): publications@ogmcs.com

First Printing: 2020

ISBN: 9798713962579

OGMC Publications
publications.ogmcs.com

Ordering Information:
Special discounts are available on quantity purchases by corporations, associations, educators, and others. For details, contact the publisher at the above listed address.

Authors' Profile

Muhammad Zeeshan Ali

PMP, PMI-ACP

Saqib Javed John

PMP, PMI-ACP, ITIL

Author of multiple books and numerous articles elaborating new dimensions of Agile framework and Traditional Project Management along with his work on Performance Management, PMO, Leadership, Team Building and Personal Motivation. He is best known for designing first of its kind "Performance Measurement Matrix" to calculate number-based performance indicators and scoring for both Software Engineering Individuals and Teams. Zeeshan is a great advocate and promoter of adaptation of Agile Methodologies, Processes and Team Skill building.

Zeeshan has over 18 years of experience of managing 100+ mid-large scale, high visibility projects in both Public and Private sectors. Experienced in managing several significant projects simultaneously and with team spread over different geo-locations.

Zeeshan has Degrees in Project Management (MS) and Computer Sciences (BS). He has been certified as a Project Management Professional (PMP) and Agile Certified Professional (PMI-ACP) by Project Management Institute (PMI), USA.

Saqib is one of the founding members and Managing Director of Organizational Governance Management Consultants (OGMC). He has professional expertise of more than 18 years of working on enterprise projects in various business domains ranging from functional organization to projectized organization.

Saqib has immense experience in developing and managing human behavior, process engineering and optimization, risk management, conflict management, performance maturity audits and policy making. This is one of the reasons he is relatable to readers of Business and management professions. He is the best known for his rapid-learning techniques and easy methods of practical implementations. He also has contributed to many anthologies. His work is helping thousands of students, teachers and professionals.

Saqib is MS (IT), certified "Project Management Professional" (PMP) and "Agile Certified Practitioner" (ACP) from Project Management Institute (PMI) USA. He is also certified in "Information Technology Infrastructure Library" (ITIL) from Exin UK, "Sun Certified Java Programmer" (SCJP) and "Sun Certified Web Component Developer" (SCWCD) from Sun Microsystems USA.

Contents

1.0 Key Points for PMI-RMP Exam

1. Key for Exam (FM-UA); (Familiarize, Memorize, Understand, Apply)

2. All Project initially based on; (Assumptions, Estimations, Hypothesis, Uncertainties, Scenarios)

3. Reasons of project Failure; (Actually Impossible, Unrealistic Objectives, Too Little thought, Lack of adaptation of organization policies and Risk Management policies)

4. Project Management Plan Benefits (FEB-L3); (Fewer Surprises, Early Identification of Gaps, Better Communication, Less Rework, Less Chaos & Fire Fighting, Lower Timeline & Reduced Cost)

5. Enterprise Environmental Factors (BAD-P2S2T2-PCM-W); (Benchmarking, Attitude, Database, Published Checklists, Published Information, Academic Studies, Industrial Studies, Threshold, Tolerance, Organization Culture, Political Climate, Fluctuations of Targeted Market, Work Authorization System) but not Physical environment

6. Organizational Process Assets (IFL-C3-RAT); (Information, Files, Lesson Learned, Concepts, Controls, Categories, Role & Responsibilities, Authority, Templates of Statement and Standards)

7. Project Documents (11), (CNS-IQ-R2D2M2); (Project Charter, Project Schedule, Project Network Diagram, Quality checklists, Issue Log, Risk Register, Stakeholders Register, Requirement Documents, Procurement Documents, Metrics, Method Statement)

8. Quality Controls (7), (HP-CS-RF2); (Histogram, Pareto Chart, Control Chart, Scatter Diagram, Run Chart, Flow Chart, Fish Bone)

9. Five Basic Reports (FPSEV); (Forecast, Progress, Status, Earned Value, Variance)

10. Contract Types; (Fixed Price, Cost Reimbursable, Time & Material)

11. Fixed Price Contracts; (Firm, with Incentive Fee, with Economic Price Adjustment)

12. Cost Reimbursement Contract; (Cost plus Fixed Fee, Cost plus Incentive Fee, Cost plus Percentage of Costs (Buyer/Seller Split of Additional Cost))

13. 5 Motivation Theories (CM3H); (Maslow (theory of needs), McClelland's (Three Needs' theory), McGregor (X&Y type), Herzberg (AKA Theory of hygiene, Two-Factor Theory), Contingency Theory)

14. Maslow's Hierarchy of Needs (BSS); Basic Needs (Biological/Physiological, Safety/Security), Social Need (Acceptance/Belonging, Respect (Self Esteem)), Self-Actualization

15. McClelland's 'Three Needs' Theory (AAP); (Achievement, Affiliation, Power)

16. Theory of X & Y people; (Y people like work & responsibility, X people don't like work and responsibility)

17. Forms of Power (PEL-R2); (Punishment, Experience, Legitimate, Reward, Referent)

18. Organization Structure Types; (Functional, Projectized, Matrix(Weak, Mix, Strong)), "Strong Functional" is not a valid organization type

19. Leadership Styles (9), (ABCD-PT-S2L); (Autocratic, Bureaucratic, Charismatic, Democratic, People Oriented, Task Oriented, Servant, Situational, Laissez Faire)

20. Communication Dimensions (11); (Formal, Informal, Official, Un-Official, Verbal, Non-Verbal, Internal, External, Vertical, Horizontal, Diagonal)

21. Communication Skills / Interpersonal Skills / Soft Skills to Manage Stakeholders, Project Manager should have qualities/skills;
    a. (G2-FLN); (Good Knowledge of Project Management Practices, Good Judgment, Flexibility, Leadership, Negotiation)
    b. (ABC-P2WR); (Active Listening, Building Trust, Conflict Resolution, Presentation, Public Speaking, Writing Skills, overcoming resistance to change)

22. Communication or Information Sharing Methods; (Pull, Push and Interactive)

23. Examples of Pull Communication method; (E-Learning, Web Site, Knowledge Repository, Designated Resource Center, Network Directory)

24. Examples of Push Communication method; (News Letter, Email, Attachments, Texting, Voice Message, Reports)

25. Examples of Interactive Communication method; (Real Time back and forth communication like, Meetings, Audio/Video Conference Call, Telephone)

26. Seven components of any Communication Model (Sender, Receiver, Message, Language, Medium, Confirmation, Feedback)

27. Fact and Risk difference; (Facts and Certainties are not Risks, Probability more than 80% is Fact)

28. What is Risk (FMU); Fundamental Reality, Matter of Perspective, Unexpected Outcome (May or may not happen, Might go Good or Bad)

29. Sources of Risk; (Natural, Man Made)

30. Risk Cycle; (Identify□ Measure (Asses & Prioritize)□ Manage (if +ve Maximize, if –ve Minimize) □ Monitor & Control

31. Measurement of Risk is done by; (Qualitative or/and Quantitative Risk Analysis)

32. Risk Models (MDM); (Risk Matrices, Decision Tree, Modeling & Simulation)

33. Modeling & Simulation Techniques; (Artificial Wave Model, Monte Carlo Simulations)

34. Factors of Risk Magnitude (5); (Probability, Impact (Severity), Frequency of occurrence, Expected Timing of occurrence, Urgency), (Note: Probability and Impact are more stronger factors than Urgency)

35. Potential Indicators of Risk (5) (TOPER); (Tools, Organization, People, Estimates and Requirements)

36. Good or Positive Risk's Characteristics;(Probability to Make Money)

37. Bad or Negative Risk's Characteristics; (Probability to Lose Money, Undesirable Events, Can Dig grave for Project if not managed properly)

38. Categories of Risk Identification Techniques; Past (Historic Reviews), Present (Current Assessment), Future (Creativity Techniques)

39. Details of Risk Identification Techniques (SAID)
    a. Status Meetings
    b. Analysis Techniques 10 (ABTCD-S2R2W) (Assumptions, Bottom-Up Analysis, Top-Down Analysis, Checklist Analysis, Decision Tree Analysis, SWOT, Sensitivity Analysis, Root Cause Analysis (Pareto/80-20), Regression Analysis, What-If Analysis)
    c. Information Gather/Group Creativity Techniques (Brain Storming, Brain Mapping, Interviews, Delphi, Nominal)
    d. Diagraming Techniques (Flow Charts, Fish Bone, Affinity, Influence)

40. What is Distribution; "Interval of Numbers" organized on their chance of occurrence

41. Probability Distribution (TUB2-NL-CD-P2); (Triangular, Uniform, Beta, Binominal, Normal, Log Normal, Continuously, Discrete, Poisson, Posterior)

42. Two common types of Bias in Risk Data; (Cognitive Bias, Motivated Bias)

43. Main Categories of Risk; (Strategic, Financial, Operational, Reputational, Compliance)

44. Types of Risks (BP-I2P2); (Business Risk, Pure Risk, Identified Risk, Potential Risk, Individual Risk, Project Risk)

45. PMBOK Risk Categories (PET-POQ); (External, Technical, Performance, Organizational, Quality, Project Management)

46. Internal Risk; (People, Process, Operations, Technology)

47. External Risks (E2-SLMP-DRT); (Environmental, Economic, Social, Legal, Market, Political, Design, Regulatory, Taxation)

48. PMBOK Risk Categories (PET-POQ); (External, Technical, Performance, Organizational, Quality, Project Management)

49. Other types of Risks (DASE2RI); (Directional, Absolute, Sovereign, Energy, Exposure, Relative, Investment)

50. Financial Risk; (Credit, Market, Liquidity)

51. People Risk (AB-FE-H2S2-T); (Availability, Background Check, Fraud, Employment Law, Health & Safety, Human Error, Skills Development, Training, Segregation of Duties)

52. Process Risk (PSF-C); (Project, Supply, Financial, Customer)

53. Operational Risk(PSF-BSL); (Political, Safety, Fraud - Business Practices, System Failures, Legal)

54. Technology Risk (SC2D2); (System performance, Capacity Planning, Change Management, Data Security, Data Integrity)

55. Risk Management Characteristics/Policy (10) (VI2S2-PC-TRN); (Valuable, Integral, Important, Systematic, Structured, Preventive, Continual Improvement, Transparent, Responsive, Natural)

56. Risk Management is not...(IS2O) (Isolated, Static, Substitute for the other project management processes, Optional)

57. Things to consider before Risk Management; (Size and Value of the Project , Stakeholder's Risk Profile (AACT) Attitude, Appetite, Culture and Tolerance)

58. Requirements for Better, Successful and Effective Risk Management (DUR4); (Drive Risk Culture from Top, Use Risk Managers, Right Level of Integration, Right Organizational Setup, Right combination of Strategic & Operational Risk Management, Right connectivity between Bottom-up and Top-down Management)

59. Risk Management provides and helps in/to (S2AFE- R2P3M2); (Strategic Decision Making, Safety Signals, Align with Value Drivers, Failure Proofing, Eye-Opener, Less Reactive, Realistic Targets, More Proactive, Predictions, Prevent Future Problems, Mistakes & Misalignments, Mechanism to "Pull everything together")

60. Risk Management Plan provides (F2M3-T6-BR); (Formats, Frequency, Methodology, Matrix, Management Intent, Timing, Tracking, Tools & Techniques, Terms & Definitions, Tolerance, Threshold, Budgeting, Roles & Responsibilities)

61. Types of Risk Management Decision (TD2); (Time-Critical (On the Run), Deliberate, In-Depth)

62. Responsible for Risk Governance; (Project Manager, PMO, Management Team)

63. Risk Governance Responsibilities (AMEO); (Awareness of all Internal & External Risks, Monitoring & Control, Ensuring Consistency, Oversight the Entire process)

64. Risk Governance Includes/provides (SP4-L2); (Standards, Policies, Procedures, Practices, Performance Measurements, Lesson Learned, Library or Cemetery of Risks)

65. Enterprise Risk Management Organizational level Benefits.... (ABC5DE2-GHI2-LPR3ST2); (Improve... Achievements, Business, Cash flow, Corporate Value, Controls, Confidence, Compliance, Decision Making, Efficiency, Effectiveness, Governance, HSE Performance, Incident Management, Insight, Learning, Proactive, Rating, Resilience, Reassuring Stakeholders, Survival, Trust, Transparency)

66. Expert Judgment is used for; (Interpretation of the data, Identify strengths and weaknesses of Tools & Techniques)

67. Risk Management Roles (Project Sponsor, Project/Risk Manager, Project Team, Risk Owner, Risk Action Owner, Risk reporter)

68. Proactive Risk Management(AT-VSD); (Automated Alerts, Preset Triggers, Visualize Information, Statistical Functions, Data Mining)

69. Risk Management contain 6 Activities: (Risk Management Plan, Identify Risks, Qualitative Risk Analysis, Quantitative Risk Analysis, Plan Risk Response, Control Risk)

70. Indicators of Risk Prioritization...(PRWT) (Probability, Risk Rating, Symptoms and Warning Signs, Time to affect a risk response)

71. Risk Register may include… (RPWT- ICU) (Identified Risks, Categorization information, Urgency Information, Prioritized List, Ranking or Scores, Trends and Results, Watch list (Non Critical Risks))

72. Stakeholder register contains Stakeholder's information related to (ICI-SARE); (Identification, Classification, Influence, Skills, Abilities, Requirements, Expectations) but not Stakeholder Management Strategy

73. Stakeholder Classification Grids; (Power/Interest Grid, Power/Influence Grid, Influence/Impact Grid)

74. Stakeholder Salience Model (PUL) and its use; has three levels of evaluation (Power, Urgency, Legitimacy) and used to Rank the Stakeholders

75. Difference between Dangerous and Demanding Stakeholders; Dangerous (who has the Power and Urgency but no Legitimacy), Demanding (Only Urgency)

76. Risk Response Strategies
    a. For Threats (A2TM/T4) (Avoid, Mitigate, Transfer, Accept)/(Terminate, Treat, Transfer, Tolerate)
    b. For Opportunities (E2SA) (Exploit, Enhance, Share, Accept)

77. Examples of Risk Transfer and Insurable Risks (Contracting, Insurance, Warranties, Guarantees, Bonds)

78. Four express guarantee categories are (DEW-P); (Design, Equipment, Workmanship and Performance (process))

79. Five components of a Legal Contract…PCO-CA (Purpose, Capacity, Offer, Consideration, Acceptance)

80. Objectives of Qualitative Risk Analysis Process;(BRE-UP) (Better understanding, Reduce the level of uncertainty, Evaluation, Urgency Assessment, Prioritization (Top to Down or form most important to least important))

81. Objectives of Quantitative Risk Analysis Process; (QDS-JIN) (Quantifying the impact/effect of the Risks in terms of Time and Cost, provides the Data on the probability of achieving objectives, help to better Justify contingency reserves, to make decisions in the presence of the current uncertainties, Sensitivity Assessment, Identify project level Risks to reduce project uncertainty, To Identify the extent of overall Project Risk, Numerical Analysis to compare with Project Baselines and to support decision making)

82. Plan risk response process Objectives; (What will be done and who will be responsible for each top risk, To enhance opportunities and to reduce threats, Risk-related Contractual)

83. Output from Plan Risk Response (P3(MCF)-AT); (Mitigation Plan, Contingency Plan, Fallback Plan, Finalized Risk Owners, Triggers and also can be (Secondary Risks and Residual Risks))

84. Objectives of Control Risk Process; (I2TEM) (To implement Risk Response Plan, Identifying New Risks, Tracking identified Risks, Evaluate & Ensure consistency and effectiveness, Ensure Compliance' Monitoring Residual Risks, Reassess & Refine', To)

85. Types of Risks Identified during Risk Management Processes (IRSE); (Identified Risks, Residual Risk, Secondary Risks, Emergent Risks)

86. Risk Response Plans (MFC); (Mitigation Plan, Contingency Plan, Fallback Plan (2nd Contingency Plan, Plan B))

87. Strategy and Actions about Risks depends on; (PAC) (Priority, Affordability and Cost Effectiveness)

88. Format of Risk Statement should be; (CCU) (Consistent, Clear and Understandable)

89. Risk can be categorized and arranged by using (4); (RBS, WBS, Project Phase, Common Root Cause)

90. Risk Ranking evaluation path; (RSR) (Risk Rating -> Risk Scoring -> Risk Ranking)

91. Risk Classification; (High, Moderate and Low)

92. Risk Attitude is driven by (PTO); (Perception, Tolerance and Other Biases)

93. Methods for Conflict Management (S2C2-FRW); (Compromise, Collaboration, Problem Solving, Smoothing, Forcing , Referent, Withdraw)

94. Contract Administrator can use following as a Contract; MPA (Purchase Order, Memorandum of Understanding, Agreement)

95. People must Involve in selecting a strategy; (SET) (Stakeholders, Experts, Team)

96. Known descriptive terms derived from Risk Analytical techniques; (SLNR-U) (Supportive, Leading, Neutral, Resistant, Unaware) but not (Non-Resistant, Aware)

97. Subsidiary Plans (9); (Scope MP, Time MP, Cost MP, Quality MP, HR MP, Communication MP, Risk MP, Procurement MP, Stakeholders MP)

98. Project Manager Job Characteristics: (Challenging, High Profile, Responsibility, Responsibility, Responsibility...Communicate, Communicate, Communicate....)

99. JURAN'S TRILOGY of continuous improvement; (Quality Planning, Quality Control, Quality Improvement)

100. Three main Baselines in Project Management are (Scope Baseline, Schedule Baseline, Cost Performance Baseline)

101. Levels of Stakeholders
    a. Major Stakeholders; (Sponsor)
    b. 2nd Level Stakeholders; (Project Manager, Project Team, Other Project Teams)
    c. 3rd Level Stakeholders; (PMO, Program Manager, Portfolio Manager, Operational Manager, Functional Manager, Legal Counsel, Government, Regulatory Authorities, Customer, Customer's customer, Different internal departments (Sales, Marketing, Quality and Procurement))

102. Group Decision Making Techniques; M-PDU (Unanimity, Majority, Plurality, Dictatorship)

103. PDM (Precedence Diagramming Method) has four kinds of logical relationship or dependences (F-S, S-F, S-S, F-F)
    a. F – S; Initiation of Successor depends upon the completion of Predecessor
    b. F – F; Completion of Successor depends upon completion of Predecessor
    c. S – S; Initiation of Successor depends upon the Initiation of Predecessor

    d. S – F; Completion of Successor depends upon Initiation of Predecessor

104. Type of Dependences (HSL/MDE); (Mandatory Dependencies (Hard Logic), Discretionary Dependencies (Soft Logic or Preferred Logic), External Dependencies (Logical Relation between Project and Non Project Activities))

105. Integrated Change Control Management includes; (Change Request, Configuration Management)

106. Parts of the Change Requests; (Corrective Actions, Preventive Actions, Defect Repair)

107. Types of changes; P2-SBD (Project Changes, Process Changes, Scope Changes, Baseline Changes, Deliverables Changes)

108. Schedule Compression Techniques; (Crashing, Fast Tracking)

109. Fast Tracking is about; (Reordering the activities, changing sequential activities into parallel activities, using the concept of Lead or overlapping, it increase Risk)

110. Crashing is about; Adding resources which results in adding Cost (adding Resources means adding Dollars)

111. Tuckman's Theory (FSNPA); (Forming, Storming, Norming, Performing, Adjourning)

112. Process Improvement Plan includes (MCB-T); (Process Matrix, Process Configuration, Process Boundaries, Target for Improved Performance)

113. Cost Benefit Analysis includes (MLM); (More Productivity, Less Rework, More satisfied Customer & Stakeholders)

114. Foundation values of Code of Ethical & Professional Conduct; (Honesty, Fairness, Responsibility, Respect)

115. Standard as formal document describes; (Norm, Methods, Processes, Procedures that are consistent and generally accepted)

116. Methodology consist on; Process, Data, Tools

117. Project is temporary but always produce; (Product, Service, Results)

118. Product's main characteristics are; (Sequential, Non-Over Lapping)

119. Product's Life-Cycle; (Idea, Market, Grows, Mature, Decline, Retired)

120. Un-Planned Trainings include; Observations, Conversations, Project Management Appraisal

121. Out Puts of five phases of Project Management Framework I-P-E&MC-C; Project Charter, Project Management Plan, Acceptable Deliverables, Archive of Project Documentation

122. Common Outputs of all processes of Planning phase is; Project Documents Update

123. Four Common Outputs of Execution and M&C are; Project Documents Update, Project Management plan Update, OPA Update, Change Request

124. Common Output of M&C for Scope, Time and Cost is; Work Performance Information

125. Output of M&C for Quality is; Quality Performance Measurements

126. Other valid terms used for closing phase are; Phase Gate, Exit Gate and Kill Point

127. Process Improvement Methods; CMMI, OPM3 and Malcolm-Bridge

128. Project Management Plan is singed by; Sponsor, Stakeholder(s) and Operations Manager

129. Project Management System is an application of; Knowledge, Skill, Tool & Techniques, Procedures and Mythologies

130. Successful project means, meeting expectations of; Sponsor, Stakeholder(s) and Customer

131. Critical Path Method is used to calculate; ES, EF, LS, LF using Forward and Backward pass technique, Project Finish Date, Activities which can slip, Activities which can't slip

132. Performance Reports includes information on; Scope, Time, Cost and Quality

133. Two most important outputs of Project Management Framework; Deliverables, Work Performance Information

134. Relations of CPM and CCM; (CPM has four relations F-S, S-F, F-F and S-S), (CCM has only one i.e. F-S)

135. Additional Buffer is also known as; Feeding Buffer

136. Preceding also known as; Predecessor

137. Initiation is also known as; Pre-planning

138. Deming is also known as; Plan-Do-Check-Act

139. Cause & Effect Diagram is also known as; Ishikawa Diagram and Fish Bone Diagram

140. Root Cause Analysis is also known as; Pareto Chart, Pareto Law, Pareto Principle, 80-20 Rule, the law of the vital few

141. Histogram is also known as; Bar Chart or Vertical Chart

142. Histogram is used to show; Frequency of occurrence (and it is used only for continuous data)

143. Resource Histogram is used for; Project Staffing, Resource Leveling, To show the utilization of Project Resources over a Time Scale

144. WBS is also known as; Information-Hub of the Project

145. Award type "Win-Lose" is also known as; Zero-Sum

146. Herzberg Theory is also known as; Motivation Hygiene Theory or Two Factor Theory (Factors that contribute to satisfaction, Factors that contributes to dissatisfaction)

147. Difference between Econometric and EVM Model used for Project Performance Forecasting; Econometric based on Assumptions while EVM based on past project performances

148. EVM includes; EV, PV, AC, Variance, Performance Measurement and Forecasting

149. Run Chart is used to show and test (HTV-(M-CTO)-O2); History of Defects, Variance, Tracking (Mixtures, Clustering, Trends, Oscillations), Outputs over Time Scale, Outcome are under control or not

150. Pareto Chart is used to show(QC-IT); Quantify, Categorize, Identify areas where to put effort, Top to Down Frequency sequence of defects

151. Run Char is also sometimes called; Control Chart

152. Root Cause Analysis includes; Problem Identification, Discovery of Under laying Issues, Development of Preventive Actions

153. Root Cause Analysis Techniques; A Fish Bone Diagram, Why-Why and How-How

154. Configuration Management includes; Identify, Status Accounting, Verify & Audit

155. Contingency Theory; Leadership (Task Oriented / Relationship Oriented), Work Environment (Stressful / Easy to work)

156. Composite Resource Calendar Includes; Availability, Capability, Skills

157. Business Case contains; Business Needs and Cost Benefit Analysis

158. Project Scope Statement includes (C2-DAR2); Constraints, Complexity, Deliverables, Assumptions, Requirements (Project & Product), Risks (High Level) and also the "Items to be excluded from the project"

159. Project Charter includes High Level Information i.e. (MO-DA3R); (High Level Milestone, Objectives, Directives, Proof of Authority, Authorize the existence of the Project, Authorize the Project Manager, Risks)

160. WBS includes following works; Project Work, Product Work and Project Management Work

161. OPM3: Organizational Project Management Maturity Model

162. PERT: Program Evaluation and Review Technique also known as 3-Point estimates, weighted average of three estimates "Most-likely", "Pessimistic", "Optimistic"

163. GERT: Graphical Evaluation and Review Technique (uses a Feedback Loops)

164. RAM: Responsibility Assignment Matrix

165. RACI (Ray-Cee): Responsibility, Accountability, Consult, Information

166. CMMI: Capability Maturity Model Integration

167. Effective Communication; Right Format, Right Impact, Right Time

168. Most of the Project Communication is related to; Project Performance, Performance Reporting

169. Four (4) Common Tool & Technique used in Planning Processes; Meetings, Expert Judgment, Analytical Techniques, Requirement Analysis

170. In short, Plan means = How + Who + When

171. Risk related communication occurs at two levels; Project Level and Activity Level

172. Compliance Ensures; Plan, Policies and Procedures are being followed

173. Suitable strategies for critical risks with high impact; Avoid, Mitigate

174. Suitable strategies for less critical & low impact risks; Transfer, Accept

175. Design means; Detailed description of Requirements and Functionalities

176. Analogous Analysis Characteristics (six); Less Time (faster than parametric), Less Cost, Less Accurate, Top Down, Based on the Expert knowledge and Historic same kind of Projects, Based on limited information

177. Communication Plan Tells; What, When and Which format

178. Communication about Risk and its handling; Open, Honest and Transparent

179. Project Charter do not contain; (Scope Statement)

180. Which skill can't be used to manage projects; (Private Speaking)

181. Which skill can't be used to manage Stakeholders; (Non-Verbal)

182. The best method, worst method to resolve the conflict and method to minimize the conflict; (Best Method: Problem Solving, Worst Method: Forcing, To Minimize Conflict: Smoothing)

183. Identified Risk, Unidentified Risk and Facts are also Known as; (Known-Unknown, Unknown-Unknown or Blind-Spots, Known-Known)

184. Unknown-Unknown and Known-Unknown Risks are dealt by; (Management Reserves, Contingency Reserves)

185. Contingency Reserves are for; (Time and Cost)

186. Number of Iterations depends upon; (Type, Value and Size of the project)

187. Probability and Impact means; (Chances of occurrence, Severity of outcome)

188. Pre-Mortem means ; (Theoretical Analysis of the project before its actual start)

189. Decision Tree Analysis are used for …. instead of….; (Individual Risk instead of Project Level Risks)

190. Risk Analysis should be the part of (GMC); (Go or No-Go decisions, Make or Buy decision, Contracts)

191. Risk Management Context is a combination of (S2); (Stakeholders Risk Attitude and Strategic Risk Exposure)

192. Exposure means; Measure of Sensitivity and Level of Risk on the Project

193. Difference between Good and Bad surprises; (Good Surprises – Helps), (Bad Surprises - Hurt)

194. Documentation of Risk Analysis provides insight; (Credibility and Reliability of Analysis)

195. Systems which helps to ensure "What work should happen in what order"; (Work Authorization System and WBS Dictionary)

196. "Who is responsible for what" is given in; (Responsibility Assignment Matrix)

197. Reviewing and Approving the Change Requests is the responsibility of; (Project Integration Management)

198. PMO Office can do following within an Organization (LADS-D(SP)-PM(AHMC)); (Lead, Audit, Direct, Support, Creating and Maintaining Documentation (Defines Standards and Policies), Project Managers (Assigning, Helping, Mentoring and Control Project Managers))

199. PMO's Audit of the project, focus most on; (Project Management Plan and Work Performance Information)

200. Who is responsible of EVM and to Identify Risks; (Everyone)

201. Risk Owners could help in (R-SP-CV); (Determine Risk Resources, To select suitable strategy and defining actions, To create Risk Response Plans (P3), Control Risks, Validate Effectiveness of Risk Reponses)

202. Responsibilities of Project Manager during in Risk Management (R-SP2-CE2); (Resources and their issues, To develop the Strategies for both Activity level and Project level Risks, Part of Procurement Negotiation, To develop Risk Responses Plans(P3), To ensure the Closure Description of every Risk in Risk Register, To select Experts for expert judgment, To manage overall Risk Exposure of the project)

203. Prompt List is also known as; (Generic List of Risk Categories)

204. Three Critical Input to identify risks at Micro and Macro level; WBS, Scope Statement and Procurement Documents

205. Brain Storming is also known as; (Free-Flow-of-Ideas, Think Aloud)

206. Qualitative Risk Analysis is also known as; (Subjective Risk Analysis, Partial Risk Analysis)

207. Techniques used for "Numerical System to evaluation and "Priority Assessment" are; (Probability & Impact Matrix, Risk Matrix, Risk Rating Matrix, Look-up-Table)

208. Watch List is also known as; (List of Non-Top Risks, List of Low-Scoring Risks)

209. Chart of Accounts is used; (To align the cost with WBS and RBS)

210. Bar Chart in Risk Management is used to show also; (Risk owner and Risk Score)

211. Risk Rating and Mapping rules are determined by; (The Organization and added in OPA)

212. Probability Distribution is used extensively in; Modeling and Simulations

213. Triangular Distribution is also known as; (3-Point Estimates)

214. Beta Distribution is also known as; PERT Distribution and this distribution is frequently used in PERT Diagram

215. Which Distributions gives more weightage to Most-Likely value; Triangular distribution, Beta Distribution

216. Formula for Triangular distribution; Average of its three parameters: (Min + Mode + Max) / 3

217. Formula for PERT distribution; (Min + (4*Mode) + Max) / 6

218. Which Distribution is mostly used in simulation and why; Triangular Distribution is most frequently used in Simulations because it's relatively easy to create from the judgment of experts

219. PERT/Beta distribution method used for; Project Scheduling

220. Which Distribution provides Better Estimates (Triangular or Uniform) and Why; Triangular Distribution provides better estimates than Uniform Distribution because 'most likely' data has more Weightage

221. Types of Triangular and Beta Distributions; Symmetrical and Asymmetrical

222. Normal Distribution is also known as; Bell-Shaped Distribution

223. In a Normal Distribution the mean is equal to; Zero (0)

224. The total area under the curve for any continuous distribution must equal to; 1 (one)

225. Continuous & Discrete Probability Distributions are used for subsequently; (1stUncertainty in Values, 2nd Events)

226. Uniform Probability Distribution can be used if; When there is no obvious value during the early concept stage of design

227. Poisson Distribution is an example of; Discrete Distribution

228. What is Log Normal Distribution; It is a special kind of Normal Distribution frequently used for Reliability Applications

229. Binomial Distribution possible outcomes; only 2 possible outcomes (Success or Failure)

230. Joint Probability means; The probability of two or more independent events occurring

231. New Risks identified during Plan Risk Responses and Control Risk process are also known as; (Emergent Risks)

232. Contingency Response Plan is also known as; (Planned Responses)

233. Triggers are also known as; (Warnings, Signals, Indicators)

234. Buyer is also known as (3); Owner, Sponsor, An Acquiring Organization

235. Seller is also known as (3); Contractor, Supplier and Service Providers

236. Critical Variance is also known as; Maximum Tolerable Variance

237. Accepted Risks also contains; (Unidentified Risks)

238. Workaround is also known as; (Reactive Actions, Unplanned Responses of Unplanned Risks)

239. Root cause analysis is also known as; Special Cause Analysis

240. Tools used for QA and QC; (Quality Audit for QA and Quality Inspection for QC)

241. What is used to separate the risks from its Cause & Effects; Risk Meta Language

242. Communication between Peer is the example of; Internal, Informal and Unofficial

243. Tools for Qualitative Risk Analysis; (Probability & Impact Matrix)

244. Tools & Techniques used during Risk Quantification; (Probabilities Tables, Decision Tree, Expected Monetary Value, Monte Carlo, Statistical Sums)

245. Liabilities of the performance contract could be; (Patent and Copy right)

246. Project Risk through liabilities comes in two forms; Breach of Contract and a Tort

247. Examples of Tort are (A2BS); (accident, assault, battery, slander)

248. Expected Value means; A measure of central tendency

249. Co-Relation means; Relation between sets of Data

250. Types of the Co-Relations are; (High Positive, Low Positive, High Negative, Low Negative)

251. RMA stands for; Risk Management Association

252. ROM stand for; Rough Order Magnitude (AKA High Level Estimates or Big Range Estimates)

253. Definitive Estimates are also known as; Accurate Estimates, Detailed Estimates, Close Variance Range (5 to 10% variance)

254. To avoid Risk, PM must consider before selecting a vendor (MES); (vendor's…Experience, Personnel skills, Material control procedures)

255. Six Questions of Risk Management; (1. What we are trying to do / achieve? 2. What might affect 3. Which are the most important that can affect 4. What we should do about them 5.Did it work 6. What Changed)

256. Autocratic Leadership style generates risks (C2M); (Low Moral, Low Commitment, Low Creativity)

257. Charismatic Leadership style generates risks; (One Man show, Team output decrease if Leader leaves, Commitments are more towards Leader rather than Goal)

258. Benefits of Laissez-Faire Leadership style (CDEF); (Coaching and Helping Team members, Leader invites team to involve in

Decision Making, Encourage Creativity & Innovation, Flexible (No Strong and Excessive Controls))

259. Advantages of Functional Organization (B2C3); (Clear Roles, Clear Communication, Clear Promotion Path, Best Controls, Business Unit Competency), but staff give priority to day-to-day work not the project work

260. Projectized Organization Characteristics; (Fast, Flexible, Dynamic, Mixed Knowledge and Experience, Focus only on completion of a project, most resources are involved in Project Work, Staff give priority to project work

261. Advantages of Matrix Organization; (Less Resource Duplication, More Better Communication Channels, Staff more Committed to the Project)

262. Cost of Conformance (PIA-GTD); is the cost of (Precautions, Inspections, Appraisal, Guidelines, Trainings, Documentation) to Improve Efficiency and to make a greater type of product

263. Cost of Non-Conformance; is the cost of Internal and External Failures (Rework, Scrap and Damaged Reputation)

264. Application of Risk Management (8) (PMOF-M2ES2); (Project's Management, Operations, Financial), Medical, Military, Space, Safety, Engineering)

265. Qualitative Risk Analysis Characteristics; (Subjective, Partial, Cost Effective, Easy to Perform, distinguish Genuine Risks from Non-Genuine Risks, decides which risks need a Response)

266. Quantitative Risk Analysis Characteristics; (Analytical, Detailed and Time Consuming)

267. Risk Rating Types; (9-Point (1 to 9), 5-Point (1 to 5) and 3-Point (1-3))

268. 3-Point subjective description; (Low, Medium, High)

269. 5-Point subjective description; (Very Low, Low, Medium, High, Very High)

270. Results of Probability and Impact Matrix; (LP-LI, HP-HI, LP-HI, HP-LI)

271. Four (4) Major keys of an Organization's Success (G-CAR); (Governance, Compliance, Audit, Risk Management)

272. Objectives of Lean strategy (DRUM); (To remove Duplication, Redundancy, Unnecessary, Misallocation)

273. Organization Goals; (A3R2L); (Aware, Align, Agile, Responsive, Resilience, Lean)

274. Famous Quality Polices/Principals; Deming (Plan-Do-Check-Act and TQM), Juran's (80-20 Pareto Law and Juran's Trilogy, Fitness for Use), Crosby (DIRFT Do it Right First Time, Zero Defect, You build Quality IN You don't Inspected IN)

275. Types of Uncertainties; (Stochastic (Possible Events Risks , May or May Not), Aleatoric (Variability, More or Less, Dice is the example), Epistemic (Ambiguity, Lack of Knowledge), Ontological (Blind Spots, Emergent Risks which occurs from nowhere, unknown & unknowable unknown))

276. Opportunities and Threats are also known as; (Good Risks - Bad Risks; Positive Risks – Negative Risks, Upside Risks – Downside Risks)

277. Difference between Risk and Risks; (Risks – individual Risks, Risk – Project Risk);

278. Different Risk Attitudes; (Averse, Seeker, Neutral, Tolerant)

279. Risk Appetite; The amount and type of Risk that an Organization is willing or need to take

280. Risk Appetite Characteristics(MIS); Internal, Multilevel, Situational or Objective (different in different situations)

281. Different Terms used in Probability Distribution assessment are (E2-TO-S2); (Experiment, Event, Trail, Outcomes, Sample Space, Sample Points)

282. Scope Baseline includes; (Scope Statement + WBS + WBS Dictionary)

283. Three plans are the backbone of the Project; (Cost Plan, Schedule Plan, Quality Plan)

284. Best and Least Efficient types of Power; (Best are 'Reward' and 'Experience, while least efficient is 'Punishment')

285. Which are not the Communication Skills; (Passive Listening, Minimizing Conflict)

286. Stakeholder outside the Performing Organization (CE2-PSF); (Customer, End User, Experts, Public, Supplier & Vendor, Fund Sources)

287. Project Constraints (7); (Scope, Time, Cost, Quality, Risk, Resources, Customer Satisfaction)

288. Pure Risks are also known as; (Insurable Risks)

289. Difference between PERT and PARETO; (PERT- 3 Point Estimate), (PARETO-80/20 Rule)

290. Triple Bottom Line for overall performance of the Organization; (Economic prosperity, Environmental quality

291. And Social capital)

292. Typical outputs expected at the end of initiating process group (4); (Project Charter is created, Project Manager is assigned, Sponsor is defined, and a High-Level scope statement put into place)

293. Two reasons for licensing the projects; (Revenue generations, Public safety)

294. Design, Lean, Resilient, Effort and Duration means; (Design – "Detailed Description of Requirements or Functionality", Lean - "Build the Muscle, Trim the Fat", Resilient - "Quick to Notice and React Back", Effort - Number of the work unit or staff hours e.g. "24 Hours", Duration – "Work in days")

295. The three layers of decomposition; (Control Account, Planning Package, and Work Package)

296. Kaizen Characteristic; (Continuous and Incremental improvement to create more value with less waste)

297. Project Sponsor's responsibilities (ABCFO); (To prepare Business Case, Charter, Authorize Project, provide Financial Resources and Own the Product when it is complete)

298. Project attributes; (Specific Purpose, Specific Results, Definite Start and End date, Temporary

299. Projects are typically created as a response to (B2TL); (Legal Requirement, Business Problem, Business Opportunity, or Technology Advance)

300. Other Valid reasons to create projects but not a primary reason (MCS); (Market Demand, Customer Need and Strategic Imperative)

301. Managing Risk means; (Finding Potential Benefits , Preventing potential problems, stopping things going wrong and help things go right, Minimize the Threats and Maximize the Opportunities, to make Threats Smaller and Opportunities Bigger)

302. Effective Delegation involves Effective Communication (4); (Clear Definition, Time Frame, Evaluation Process and Expected Results)

303. Responsible for transferring more than 90% of your message (BVPT); (Body Language, Volume, Pitch, Tone)

304. Project Management Information System (PMIS) cab be; (Manual or a High Tech system, combination of Technical and Non-Technical tools, used by various project participants to store and distribute Project Information, utilized to send right information to the right people in a timely and appropriate manner)

305. Two (2) ways to have a highly organized effective meeting; (Creating & Publishing an Agenda, knowing who is the in-charge of the meeting)

306. Type of Estimates; (Budgetary Estimates are used for Small Duration projects, Phase Estimates are use used for Long Duration projects, Detailed Estimates for Near Term work, High Level Estimates for the Future Term work)

307. Type of Costs are; [Direct Cost (only for the project), Indirect Cost(for other projects or departments also), Fixed Cost (consistent throughout the project)and Variable Cost (Fluctuate based on Quantity or Time)]

308. Purchase Order is an example of; (Unilateral Contract, Firm Fixed Price Contract)

309. The Purchase Order (Firm Fixed Price Contract) is typically used for the items that are; (Standard, Non-Customized and Non-Negotiable)

310. Two things that must be done before closing a contract; (Validation of Terms and Condition and Formal Acceptance of the Contract)

311. Three (3) must contained items for each Contract; (Contract itself, Approved Changes, and the Formal Acceptance)

312. Standard terms and conditions are typically part of a template and often addresses; (Payment options, Intellectual property rights, Sub-Contracting)

313. Advantages of using a Qualified Sellers List, ("Pre-Qualified Vendors", "Meet your industry standards", "Compatible with your company's processes") But not "Provides contracts without negotiations"

314. Bottom-up analysis gives…but; (great Clarity, more Accuracy in estimations) but took great Time to create

315. Tree Analysis; Decision Tree Analysis, Fault Tree Analysis (Failure Mode and Effect Analysis (FMEA))

316. Crisis Management characteristics; (High Cost, Embracing and Time Consuming)

317. Best assets for Risk Management; (Ideas and Information possessed by people)

318. The project manager is responsible for [PE-M&C-PD] [P-E(DO)-M&C(S2O)-P(CM)-D]; everything (Planning, Execution

(Organizing, Directing), Manage & Control (Stakeholder, Scope, Objectives), Team Performance (Coaching, Motivating), Delivery of Results But may not always control staff

319. Advantages of Projectized Environment; (Single focus Optimization, Focus on the project work without the distraction of departmental work)

320. In Projectized Environment, Project Manager is responsible for; (Resources and their issues)

321. Project Management and Quality Management both focus on; (Management Responsibility, Continuous Improvement, Prevention over Inspection, Customer Satisfaction)

322. The Contract Administrator's main responsibility is to protect; (Integrity and purpose of the contract)

323. The project manager and team should create; (Project management plan, WBS)

324. Operations Means; (Ongoing Management, Maintenance and Support)

325. The typical role of Senior Management; (To Help & Support the project, To resolve resource and other conflict) but not to resolve the issue related to "Level of Authority"

326. Staffing Management Plan contains; (Staffing Management related Items, Needs and Rules that define how to get people on the team)

327. Staffing Management Plan helps to establish (AER4); (Acquire staff, Ensure Compliance & Safety, Resource Calendars, Recognition, Rewards, Release Plan)

328. Management Styles; (Director, Visionary)

329. "Identify Risk Process" Objectives are to (9) L-(POST)2: (Long & Comprehensive List, Potential Risks, Determine Risks by Project level and by Activity level, Open & Honest identification, Risks which can affect project objectives, minimize Subjectivity, get consensus from Stakeholders, Collect Risk Tolerance and Threshold information, Control the project and reduce the project Time & Cost)

330. During Interviews ask questions, (1st Open-Ended questions, then Prepared questions, then Follow-up questions and clarify responses)

331. Interview is a very effective tool used to (CRU2); (Collect information, Uncover New Risks, Obtain an understanding of Unfamiliar parts of the project, Risk Assessment especially from experienced people)

332. Delphi Technique Advantage & Disadvantage is; (No Group Pressure, Time consuming)

333. Delphi Technique is also known as; "Anonymous Consensus"

334. Delphi Technique main highlights; (Anonymous, Consensus, Experts, Questioner)

335. Nominal Group Technique main highlights; (Open, Consensus, Selective Group of People, Nomination & Voting)

336. Nominal Group Technique also known as; ("Group Consensus" or "Group Thinking")

337. Difference between Delphi & Nominal; (Secrete Consensus of Experts, Open Consensus of Selective Group)

338. Qualitative Risk Analysis creates/deals with; (Watch List, Rating, Risk Rating Matrix, Ranking, Trends)

339. Risk Data Quality Assessment is a tool used to check; (Reliability, Accuracy, Understanding)

340. Rating is used to produce; (Risk Rating Matrix, Ranking)

341. Size of Watch List depends upon; (Stakeholder's Risk Tolerance, Low Tolerance will cause smaller Watch List)

342. What is RBS; (Graphical illustration of Risk Scoring)

343. Factors that can help to organize Risk Responses in a better way; (Urgency Level, Categorization, Scoring)

344. These two are not the best examples of Risk Categories; (Project Management Process Groups and Triple Constraints)

345. Projects and Operations share following characteristics; both are .... (performed by People, Constrained by Limited Resources, performed to achieve organizational objectives)

346. Mirror Probability & Impact Matrix also known as; (Double Matrix and Butterfly Matrix)

347. Objective of Modeling & Simulation; (Simulations translate uncertainties into their potential impacts on the project and Modeling will translate impacts into economic terms of analysis)

348. Warranties for the Product Insufficiency is also known; Product Re-Cost

349. Risk Response should be (ICT); (Innovative, Creative and Timely)

350. Avoid or Exploit Response Strategies Characteristics (TE2A); (Aggressive, Expensive, Eliminating Uncertainties and Time consuming, however this should be the first strategy considered)

351. Avoid means; (Eliminating the Threat by eliminating the cause, Execute the project in a different way)

352. Transfer or Share means; (Allocate, Assign or Outsource the work offshore)

353. Share means; Collaboration, Partnership or Joint Venture to maximize the opportunity

354. Accept Response strategy; (You Act after Risk Occurs ("If and When"))

355. Active Acceptance; (Accepted with planned responses (Contingency Plan and Contingency Reserves), Monitoring)

356. Passive Acceptance; (Accepted without planned responses)

357. Contingent Plan is also known as; Active Acceptance

358. Accepted Risks includes; (Identified Risks (Residual Risks also known as Un-Mitigated Risk, Left-Over Risks), Unidentified Risks)

359. Secondary Risks also known as; ("By-Product" of Risk Responses)

360. Which Risks can be the output of Plan Risk Response Process; (Secondary and Residual Risks)

361. Difference between Implicit and Explicit Risk Management; (Implicit deals with High Level & Project Risks, Explicit deals with Detailed & Individual Level Risks)

362. In Risk Management always keep monitoring (3); Watch List, Residual Risks, Triggers

363. Monitoring means; (Oversee the Project Performance and Project Activities)

364. During M&C process, purpose of considering performance information is; (To Collect, Measure and Interpret information)

365. There are two major reasons when Risk Reassessment occurs; (when New Risk identified and when changes occur on the project)

366. Risk Reassessment involves; (Risk Identification, Qualitative Risk Analysis, Quantitative Risk Analysis and Risk Response planning)

367. When to do Risk-Reassessment; (New Risks, Existing Risks if SPI less than or equal to 0.7, changes occur in the project)

368. Risk Audit are used; To examine and verify the effectiveness of Risk Management activities; (but not to identify additional risks)

369. Close Project or Close Phase Process includes (3); (Lesson Learned, Project Archives, Release of Resource)

370. Benefits of Proactive Quality Management (3); (Increase Processes Consistency, Increase Profits, Decreases the need for warranty support)

371. Tool & Technique used for decomposition or categorization of Risks; Influence Diagram and Cause & Effect Diagram (Ishikawa)

372. Use of Cause & Effect Diagram (Fish Bone / Ishikawa) RED-IQ; (To show Relationship between causes and their effects, To Evaluate Causes and Sub Causes of a problem, Decomposition or categorization of risk, To Isolate the problem, Quality Tool used in Quality & Risk Management)

373. Milestone Chart is used; (for Executive Reporting, To present where project stands, to define the completion of a series of activities)

374. Define Activity Process produces; Activity List, Milestone List

375. Types of the Control Limits; (Upper Specification Limit, Upper Control Limit), USL always > than UCL

376. "Line of Best Fit" is used; to estimate Data Values

377. "Fitness for use" means; To satisfy the Real Need of the customers and stakeholders

378. Seven Run Rule Violation; Seven consecutive data points on one side

379. Charts and their use; Charts are the Graphical Representation and used for Technical Analysis

380. Flow Charts shows; The Logical Steps or Logical order

381. Variable means; Something that you can measure

382. Difference between Variable, Attribute and Data/Value; (Height/Depth, Meter/Kilometer, 5/100)

383. Difference between Criteria and Value; Criteria could be a Regulation but value can't be

384. Difference between the "Sample Testing" and "Population Testing"; "Sample Testing" is not very thorough, "Population Testing" tests everything and it is recommended for only expensive products

385. Sample Testing Characteristics (3); Quicker, Less Expensive, and Less Destructive

386. A Gantt chart is also known as; Logic Bar Chart and Time Graph, showing duration of the project activities

387. Project Organization Chart is also known as; Resource Breakdown Structure

388. Project Organization Chart displays (3); (Organization Structure, Reporting Relationship and Usability of all Resources)

389. The scatter diagram shows; Relationship or lack of Relationship between two variables

390. Standard Deviation shows; How far data from their mean

391. Difference between Run Chart and Control Chart; (Run Chart presents "Trending", Control Chart represents "Stability")

392. What is the Influence Diagram? Show how the elements of a system influence each other

393. What is the Affinity Diagram? Is a method to identify additional risks and categories on project

394. Risk Management Documentation is a paramount that provides; Insight on the Reliability and Credibility of the analysis

395. Project Documents are also known as; Project Files or Supporting Documents (which are not included in Project Plan)

396. Project Documents records; what decisions were made, what changes were approved, what occurred during the project

397. Project Documents improves; Cross-Team and Stakeholders Communication

398. What is the Cross-Functional Work Environment; utilizes all groups across a company (To take advantage of the knowledge and skills available)

399. Who is the stakeholder; anyone actively involved in or impacted, negatively or positively, by the project

400. Stakeholders Life Cycle; (Identify Early, Establish their Needs, Communicate throughout the Project)

401. Issue related to Stakeholders are managed in; (Manage Stakeholders Engagement)

402. Stakeholder management is; How you put communication into practice

403. Stakeholder's Power and Interest Grid effects and responses; (HP-HI -> Close Management, LP-LI -> Just Watch and Monitor, HP-LI -> Keep Satisfied, LP-HI -> Keep Informed)

404. 'Stakeholder Salience Model (PUL)' will result in grouping Stakeholders into eight (8) categories;
    a. P. Dormant
    b. U. Demanding
    c. L. Discretionary
    d. PU. Dangerous
    e. UL. Dependent
    f. PL. Dominant
    g. PUL. Definitive
    h. Non or Potential Stakeholders

405. Latent stakeholders: One attribute, Low salience

406. Expectant stakeholders: Two attributes, Moderate salience

407. Definitive stakeholders: All three attributes, High salience

408. Stakeholder Engagement Assessment Matrix presents; Variance between current and expected levels of engagement

409. The Project Manager role is evolving from its focus on (OPD-CM3); Organizing, Planning, Directing, Coaching and Motivating, "Evolving Team Performance", "Managing key Stakeholder Expectations", (but not Mentoring, Cross-Training)

410. The Tools to minimize the conflicts; (Ground rules, Group norms, and Project management practices)

411. Risk Tolerance associated with project constrains; Scope, Time, Cost and Quality

412. High Tolerance means; Less sensitive and less willing to spend money to control risks

413. The word Threshold means; "How much is too much"

414. What is the Quality (AB); It's an Attitude and Behavior, it's about increasing the Depth and Breadth

415. Risk Maturity (AA); Approach and Attitude to meet specific needs of the situation

416. What helps to minimize, control and eliminate gold plating; (WBS and Work Authorization System)

417. What is WBS and its Use; (Tool used for Hierarchical Representation and Structured Analysis of the project work)

418. Adjourning means; Completing the task and breaking up the team (in some texts referred to as Mourning)

419. Create WBS Process is used; (Decompose the Project Work or Deliverables into Work Packages and Activities)

420. WBS is a Communication Tool used for (5) H2S-PER; (Hierarchical Representation, Structured Analysis, Planning and Controlling of Project work, Establish and Justify Resource, Time & Cost, Helps the project team to understand their role and buy-in on the project, WBS is the most effective tool to Ensure all Risks are identified)

421. What is "100% Rule"; "All efforts associated with any Deliverable or Work package should be included in WBS"

422. During the create WBS process the team can also create; (Risk Breakdown Structure, Resource Breakdown Structure and Bill of Materials); but not the Communication Breakdown Structure

423. We can add to or derived from WBS; Time (Schedules), Cost (Budgeting), Resource (Staffing) and Relationship

424. The Tool/Technique used to create WBS is; Decomposition

425. "Bill of Materials" or "Bill of Quantities" lists (CAS); Components, Assemblies, and Sub-Assemblies used to build service or product of the project

426. Resource Breakdown Structures show (ART-U); Resource's Alignment, Type, Reporting Relationship, Usability

427. Reviewing Peaks & Valleys of "Resource Allocation Chart" and making adjustment is known as; "Resource Leveling"

428. WBS Dictionary consist of documenting; (Scope Baseline, Work Packages, Control Accounts, Listing the organizations responsible for completion of the work)

429. "Define Scope" process determines; "Project Scope Statement"(AKA 'Scope Statement or' 'Summary of Intent', what the project will do, include, and exclude)

430. Use of "Control Scope process"; this process ensures that deliverables reflect the needs of the customer

431. Difference between "Design" scope of work and "Functionality" scope of work respectively; (Buyer knows exactly what is needed and wants no variance from the specifications) and (shows 'General Functional Specifications' that the outcome of the project needs to have when complete)

432. Earned value deals with and shows the status of; Scope, Time, and Cost of the project

433. The tools and techniques used during the Define Scope process are; Expert Judgment, Product Analysis, Alternatives Identification, and Facilitated Workshops but not Requirements Documentation

434. Work Authorization System tells; Certain Work will be done at what time and in which order

435. Result of "Plan Human Resource Management" process could be (ORS); Organization Chart, Roles & Responsibilities Assignments, Staffing Management Plan

436. What is Risk Breakdown Structure; Hierarchal Representation of Risk Categories, Framework to Identify Risks

437. Risk Categorization means; Grouping the Risks under Common Source

438. Matrix Organization characteristics; More than one Boss and More than one Project

439. Weak Matrix Organizations Characteristics; Limited availability of Resources, Part-time role of Project Manager

440. Functional Manager Characteristics and Role; like HRM or Accounts Manager, have Permanent Staff, Clear Directives, Runs Department or Area of Business, To provide Subject Matter Experts (SME)

441. Type of Benefits; "Fringe" and "Perks" are the types of benefits to motivate but 'Perks' are not for everyone

442. Project Team is responsible for; to Identify the stakeholders and their requirements, to execute Project Management plan

443. A team would typically be involved in; Risk Management, Budgeting and Scheduling but not in Information Distribution Plan

444. The key Tools and Techniques of the "Acquire Project Team" process are; Acquisition, Negotiation, Pre-assignment, virtual teams

445. Colocation is the process of putting personnel closer that helps in; Team Building, Project Communication

446. 'Performance Reviews' are not; Team Building or Team Developing process

447. Difference between Risk and Issue: (Risk and Issue are Different and should be managed differently, Risk in Future while issue in Present, Cost of Risk Management is less than the cost of Issue Management, Issue Log is used to Track and Manage Issues/problems while Risk Register is used for Risks, a detailed "Process Improvement Plan" can be used to fix an issues)

448. "Unforeseen Minor Problem" is also known as "Issue"

449. About the "Conflict Log"; is not a valid terminology, as conflicts are also logged in the Issue Log

450. Expert Types could be; Technical Experts, Risk Experts and Project Management Expert

451. Role of Experts in Risk Management; To spot a Risk mile away, to determine the level of probability & Impact for the specific identified risks, To provide simple solution,

452. Many factors can affect judgment; Experience, Personal Interest and Bias

453. Difference between Cognitive Bias and Motivated Bias; Cognitive Bias is due to difference in Perception, Motivational Bias is biasing the results in one direction or another

454. Contingent planning should include; Schedule Alternatives, Work around, Management of contingency budget and an Assessment of project shutdown liabilities

455. Contingency Reserves are identified based on; Calculations and Reasoning

456. Contingency reserves are used to deal with; Planned Risks, Known Unknown, Identified Residual Risks, Future Situations

457. while making changes in the project, Project Manager will be the most concerned with; Scope and Schedule impact

458. A change in the market (+ve/-ve) has the highest impact especially for; Complex Projects

459. Output of Change Control System is; "Approved Changes"

460. New Risks canotn be generated from; Change Request, Scope Creep, Extra Features, Gold Plating

461. Extra Features are also known as; Risk Laden Features of Scope Creep

462. The outputs of Validate Scope are; Accepted Deliverables and Change Requests

463. Control Scope is used to; Review Change Request, then Approve or Reject change request

464. The purpose of a Change Control Board (CCB) is to; Control changes by approving necessary and rejecting unnecessary changes

465. Corrective and Preventive actions are implemented based on the feedback of; Monitoring and Controlling Process group

466. Corrective Actions are used in order to; bring performance back in line with Project Management Plan

467. Corrective Actions & Preventive Actions are associated with; Cost and Time

468. Defect Repairs is related to; Quality

469. Not the Part of Project Plan; Corrective Actions and Project Documents

470. Baselines don't get effected by; Corrective Actions, Preventive Actions or Defect Repairs (Scope Change effect the Baseline)

471. Main output of Monitoring and Controlling; Corrective Action

472. Corrective Actions and Preventive Actions are the part of respectively; Control Risk Process, Root Cause Analysis

473. Corrective Actions and Preventive Actions are deal with the risks respectively; already occurred, not occurred yet

474. Proactive Approach; Prevention versus inspection (i.e. to eliminate potential defects from the process)

475. AC, PV and EV shows respectively; Cost, Time, Scope

476. Performance Indexes and Performance Repots will help you to check respectively; To check performance, How risks actually affect your project

477. Schedule performance index (SPI) shows; the rate at which the schedule is progressing

478. Cost performance index (CPI) shows; the rate of spending on the project

479. To Complete Performance Index (TCPI) shows; The efficiency needed to complete remaining work

480. Estimate to complete (ETC) shows; The remaining amount to be spent on a project

481. What is BCR; Benefit Cost Ratio, It considers the Benefit and Cost of an initiative

482. To calculate the EAC; Need to calculate CPI first

483. To calculate the CPI; Nee to calculate EV and AC first

484. Variance Report shows; The difference between Baseline and Actual

485. Cost Variance (CV) shows the difference between; Planned Cost and what was paid for it

486. Forecast Report shows; What is getting ready to be done on the project

487. Transformational Opportunity evolves through; The comparing current Status with Future Status

488. "Benefit Cost Ratio (BCR) of 0.90:1" means; Less Revenue than the Cost

489. EVM & EVA are Quantitative measures used to; Forecast Deviation, Compare Project Execution with Project Plan Baselines, Understanding the past and predicting the future

490. EMV (Expected Monitory Value) is used; to find the Expected Profit or Loss

491. Synergy means; To add up two values and sum is greater than the individual

492. EVM is; like a Rear Mirror to see past performance, is a Cost Technique for measuring the progress of a project, helps in managing risks

493. Calculations regarding Variance depends on; PV

494. Calculations regarding Performance depends on; EV

495. "The Weighted Milestone Approach"; Reporting periods over Two or more in length

496. "Fixed Formula Progress Approach" known as; Partial Credit Approach, here reporting periods are less than two

497. The 30%/70% Rule; is an example of Fixed Formula Progress Reporting. Activity starts given 30%, will not receive the remaining 70% until it is fully complete.

498. "Status Report" presents; Overall state of the project

499. "Progress Report" presents; what has been completed since the last reporting period

500. "Earned Valued Report" presents; state of the Schedule, Budget and Scope of the project at various points in time.

501. Risk of the Central Activity greatly increase on; Convergence and Divergence Path

502. Project Schedule is a combination of; Activity Lists, Milestone List, Network Diagrams, Gantt Charts

503. Network Diagram is also known as; Dependency-Sequenced Organization of Project Activities

504. Project Schedule Network Diagram is used to show; Sequencing of the Project Activities, Relationship between tasks and their durations, helpful in Risk identification and Simulation,

505. Similar techniques used to represent project graphically; Network Diagram, PERT and CPM

506. "Time-Scaled Schedule Network Diagram"; Once Dates are assigned to each activity of a Network Diagram

507. 'Slack' means; Flexibility with an Activity on a Network Diagram

508. Slack is calculated by; (subtracting F-F or S-S) either the late finish (LF) from the early finish (EF) or the late start (LS) from the early start (ES)

509. Slack can be; Any number +ve if ahead of schedule, -ve if behind schedule or Zero

510. Which Network Diagram Technique don't use 'Dummies'; AON (but used in AOA)

511. "Lead" means: Planned Acceleration, Starting the Successor Activity before the finish of Predecessor Activity

512. "Lag" means; Planned Delay, Slipping on the Finish Date of the project

513. Lead & Lag value nature; Lead is a –ve number to Network Diagram Lag is a +ve number to Network Diagram

514. Example of Elapse Time; (Elapse Time of the Project is "3 weeks", while work routine is 2 days per week)

515. Communication and Management Tools; WBS, Network Diagram

516. The longest path on the project is called; Critical Path which could be more than one

517. Difference between CPM and CCM; CPM emphasizes Task Order and Rigid Scheduling, CCM emphasizes Resource Flexibility and Leveling, Critical Path is without Resource while

Critical Chain is with resources, Critical Chain Method we can do after we do Critical Path

518. Critical Path with Resources is also known as; "Resource Constraint Critical Path"

519. Assumption should be; Reasonable and derived from experience and knowledge

520. The most dangerous assumption in the projects deals with; Information Transfer

521. "Del-Fa-i" refers to; a place in old Greece

522. Deming's Total Quality Management philosophy advocates an approach to quality that is; Proactive, Utilizes Leadership and Accountability and promotes Continuous Improvement

523. The evolution of Leadership and Managerial style (DCFS); Directing ---> Coaching ---> Facilitation ---> Supporting

524. Difference between American & Japanese style of Decision making and Accountability; American-Individual and Japanese-Group

525. More formal checkpoints include Go/No-Go decisions made during; Perform Qualitative Risk Analysis and Plan Risk Response Processes

526. Risk-Related contract decisions are required for; Control Risks process

527. Project Life Cycle is a; collection of Sequential or Overlapping Project Phases

528. Project Life Cycle varies depending on; Size, Value & Type of the Project (Product goes through same Life Cycle)

529. One Product Life Cycle can have; multiple Project Life Cycles

530. The Project Management Life Cycle (PMLC) is most similar to; Plan-do-Check-Act

531. Difference between Project Life Cycle (PLC) and Project Management Life Cycle (PMLC); PMLC is a Project Management Methodology and a Piece of the project. But PLC is the process of completing the work of the project

532. The very last activity on the project completion is; "Release Resource" and then "closing the project"

533. Validate scope compares; Scope with Results to get formal acceptance

534. Difference between Validate Scope and Control Scope; 1st obtaining Formal Acceptance, 2nd the correctness of the work

535. A project can be closed when; Runs out of money, Completes scope validation and when get cancelled

536. To run simulation you need; Model and Input Data, mathematical calculations and computers

537. Simulation is used to evaluate; Effect of risks on the project, to predict how project will perform

538. Project Documents also known as; Project Files

539. Project Documents do not contains; Negotiations Parameters (unless they were associated with other project documentation)

540. Risk Maturity Level comes with; the Iterative Lesson Learned

541. Post project meetings are to evaluate; Successes and Failures, What went good and bad that would result in "Lesson Learned"

542. Lessons learned is a source often used for making; Assumptions and help projects in the future run more efficiently

543. Mandatory dependency; Required and internal to the organization or project

544. Discretionary dependency; Utilizing options in completing or working with

545. External Dependency; is a factor outside the organization's control

546. Statistical Independence; Not related to occurrence of the other

547. Types of Depreciation; Standard Depreciation and Accelerated Depreciation

548. "Accelerated Depreciation" examples; Double Declining Balance and sum of the Digits

549. Mutual Exclusivity means; that only one choice can be selected. e.g. delivering quickly and minimizing shipping charges

550. Life-Cycle cost or Whole-Life Cost refers to; Total Cost of Ownership

551. Maintenance activities are categorized into four classes (APCP): (Adaptive, Perfective, Corrective, Preventive), The survey showed that around 75% of the maintenance effort was on the first two types

552. Type of SOPs; Check List, Hierarchical Steps, Linear Flow Charts, Branching Flow Charts, Annotated Pictures

2.0 Important Formulas

1.   Pareto = 80/20 Rule

2.   SD = (PS-OP)/6

3.   Formula of Variance in Beta Distribution using PERT approximations = ((PS-OP)/6) 2 OR (SD)2

4.   PERT Analysis or Three Point Estimate = (PS+4ML+OP)/6

5.   PV = Planned % completed x BAC

6.   EV = Actual % completed x BAC

7.   SV = PV – EV

8.   CV = PV – AC

9.   SPI = EV / PV

10. CPI = EV / AC

11. CPI>1 means overspending

12. SPI<1 means behind schedule,

13. SPI>1 means ahead of plan schedule (faster than planned)

14. EAC = BAC / CPI.

15. Sigma 1,2,3,6: (68.26, 95.46, 99.78, 99.99)

16. PERIL is (Project Experience - Risk Information Library)

17. FMEA = Failure Mode and Effect Analysis

18. AON = PDM

19. AOA = ADM

20. Risk Score = Probability * Impact

21. Opportunity = Probability x Gain

22. Threat = Probability x Loss

23. EMV = Probability x Investment

24. EMV = Probability x MV, it's used to calculate expected profits or losses

25. EMV = Sum of (all probabilities x impact)

26. EMV can be calculated for one/many risks with same formula Probability x Impact

27. Project milestones can be found in Project Plan Schedule

28. Project Schedule = Critical Path Duration + Contingency Reserves + Management Reserves

29. Project Budget = Cost of Activities + Contingency Reserves + Management Reserves

30. Management Reserves are not the part of Project Cost baseline and Schedule baseline

31. Root Cause = Underlying Risks

32. Standard Deviation will show how far data from their mean

33. Profit = Revenue - Expenses

34. Profit = Revenue - (Fixed cost + Variable cost)

35. Standard deviation = Square Root ((Each Number – Mean)2 / Number of Values)

36. Float or Slack = LF-EF or LS-ES

37. Sum of all probabilities must be equal to 1.0 or 100%

38. Bad Night produce Bad Days, Good Days produce Good Nights

39. Never put vision and money in the same pocket

3.0   Important Exam Tips

1. Usually people stop reading a day before exam but we must advise that please do not stop and keep revising the things as its very important to revise even those things which you know very well.

2. Don't invest time on such questions where you find very long descriptions or the questions giving you impression of difficulty and confusion. To manage such question, select any better option and put that question(s) on revision this way you can keep yourself away from going under the time pressure.

3. In order to give the right answer, you must be very sure about the three wrong answers, more or less this is the only way to give the confirmed right answer.

4. In Test/Exam room, you will get blank papers with couple of led pencils, use first 15 mins (i.e. Exam Tutorial Time) to write down the key points and formulas given in cheat sheet.

5. Must attempt the calculations based questions even if it takes little more time than the average because on such questions you will know there and then that your answer is right or wrong.

6. Keep concentrating on questions and don't eye much on the time clock, check your velocity only after 20 or 40 or 50 questions. It's a high speed exam, even seconds are important, analyzing the answering speed again and again will be time wasting and keep you under pressure.

7. Read well the question and all answers, before deciding the correct answer, if you are confused between 2 very close options then read the question again at least two times because usually solution of that ambiguity is hidden in question.

8. Try to reach at testing center one hour earlier than your exam time because testing center staff will also give you brief regarding exam rules etc. along with the few standard tips, listen to them even if you are already aware with rules/tips.

Other Books from OGMC Publications

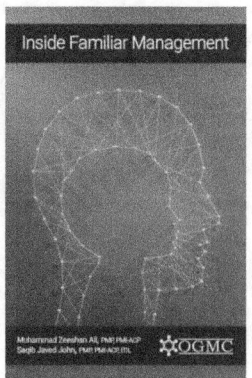